EXPLORING HISTORY

AFRICA

ISIMEME IBAZEBO

Belitha Press
In association with the Royal Geographical Society

Foreword

Many animals, birds and fish regularly travel over great distances. What sets people apart is the ability to explore and discover. An explorer is someone who is curious about the world and if you are curious enough to read this book then you too have become an explorer.

Exploring is not just about getting into a plane or sailing on a boat to a place you have never been before – you have to record what you see, listen to the people you meet and learn about the place you find. This book follows in the footsteps of all good explorers by discovering the people, history and countryside of the land before it was 'discovered' by outside peoples as well as telling tne stories of the adventurers who travelled there for the first time.

Explorers have travelled all over the world and have been helped throughout the centuries by the inhabitants of the lands they visited. People have shown outsiders their homes, helped them carry their loads, paddled their canoes, showed them amazing animals and often housed, clothed, fed, rescued and cured them. This book tells you about these people as well as the explorers they helped or fought with.

Travellers have explored the world for many different reasons. Early adventurers like Marco Polo (1254-1324) and Ibn Battuta (1304-1364) journeyed with trading caravans. Christopher Columbus (1451-1506), Ferdinand Magellan (1480-1521), Captain James Cook (1728-1779) and John Franklin (1786-1847) were sent by governments to investigate the geography of the world. Other explorers were merchants, scientists, colonialists, artists, adventurers, naturalists or even conquerors like Francisco Pizarro (1475-1541) who destroyed the Inca Empire that he discovered.

The Royal Geographical Society is proud to support the *Exploration Into* series of books. Ever since it was founded in 1830, the RGS has helped and inspired famous explorers like Robert Scott (1868-1912) and Dr David Livingstone (1813-1873). Today, the RGS helps modern-day explorers climb the world's mountains, walk across its deserts, cycle through its continents, sail up its rivers, dive deep under the oceans and discover the scientific secrets of nature. We invite you to pick up *Exploration Into* and start your own journey of discovery . . .

DR JOHN HEMMING, *Director and Secretary, Royal Geographical Society, London*

The moment at which Henry Morton Stanley finds Dr David Livingstone four years after his disappearance. It was at this point that Stanley uttered the famous words 'Dr Livingstone, I presume?'

Contents

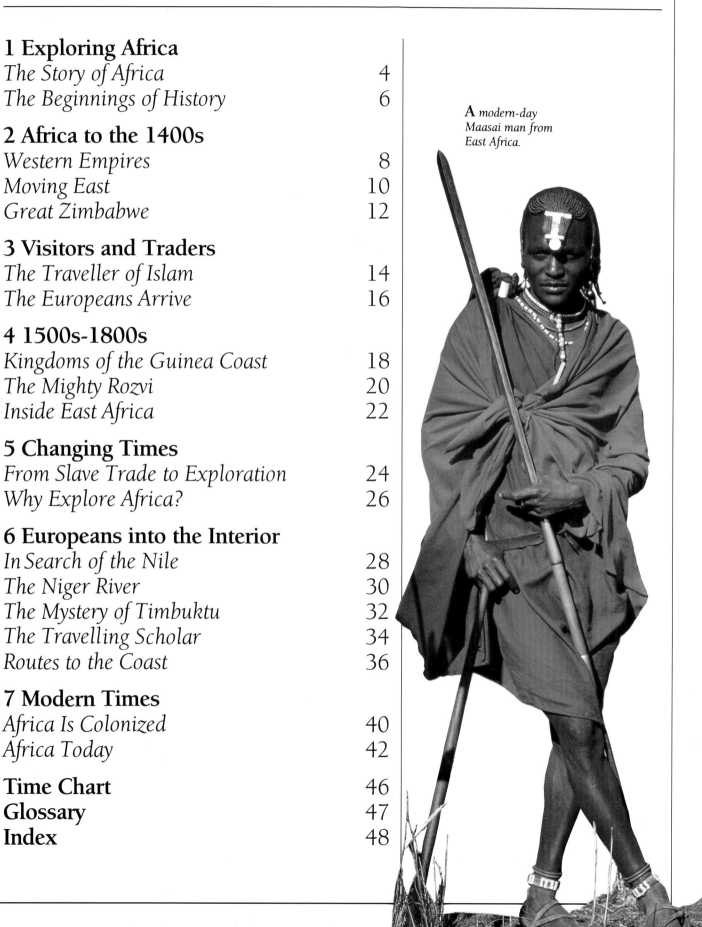

A *modern-day Maasai man from East Africa.*

Tangiers • Algiers • • Tunis

Marrakesh • Fez ATLAS MOUNTAINS
MOROCCO

Mediterranean Sea

• Tripoli

• Cairo

EGYPT

LIBYAN DESERT

NUBIAN DESERT

Red Sea

• Taghaza

Sahara Desert

SONGHAY EMPIRE

GHANA EMPIRE

• St Louis

MALI EMPIRE

• Timbuktu

• Gao

• Djenné

• Ségou

MOSSI STATES

ASANTE EMPIRE

DAHOMEY

Niger River

HAUSA STATES

• Kano

YORUBA STATES
OYO
BENIN EMPIRE

• Agades

BORNU

Lake Chad

Nile River

White Nile

Blue Nile

• Massawa

• Gondar

ETHIOPIA

CONGO BASIN

BUNYORO EMPIRE
BUGANDA EMPIRE

RWANDA

Zaïre River (Congo)

KONGO

• Luanda

Lake Victoria

Lake Tanganyika

▲ Mount Kenya

MAASAI PEOPLES

Mount Kilimanjaro ▲

Lake Malawi

Zambezi River

ROZVI EMPIRE • Great Zimbabwe

Namib Desert

KALAHARI DESERT

Orange River

• Mogadishu

• Mombasa

• Zanzibar

• Kilwa

• Quelimane

MADAGASCAR

INDIAN OCEAN

ATLANTIC OCEAN

• Cape Town

Cape of Good Hope

Over 670 million people live in Africa, in about 800 **ethnic** groups, each with their own language and culture. Africa is covered by desert, grassland and forest. The largest desert in the world, the Sahara, covers almost all of northern Africa. One of the world's longest rivers, the Nile, flows for almost 6,400 kilometres through north-eastern Africa.

Temperatures in Africa vary from region to region. The highest temperature in the world of 58°C was recorded in Libya in 1922. Rainfall also varies around the continent. Some areas, like the Sahara and Namib deserts, receive no rain for six or seven years. Along the west coast however, rain tends to fall all year round. Parts of Africa also have a dry season (when very little rain

falls) and a rainy season (when lots of rain falls). Zaire in Central Africa has a rainy season from October to May, but in the Gambia the rainy season is from July to October.

Africa has thousands of species of mammals, reptiles, birds, plants and fish. The rain forests of West and Central Africa contain hundreds of trees, from oil palms and mahogany trees to mangroves that line the coasts.

A map showing the geography of Africa and some of the kingdoms and empires of Africa up until 1800.

The dotted lines represent the boundaries of the modern-day states of Africa. Look at page 43 of this book for more detail.

1 Exploring Africa

The Story of Africa

African history is fascinating. We have all heard about the great Pharaohs of Egypt, with their magnificent tombs and burial ceremonies. But how many of us know about the ancient empires of West Africa? The first of these great kingdoms, Ghana, was powerful from 300 CE for about a thousand years (see page 8). Ghana was so rich that the dogs in the king's palace wore collars made out of gold.

Arab Scholars

In the tenth century, Arab **scholars** began to write about the great wealth of the African kingdoms. Some of them, such as Ibn Battuta (see pages 14-15), actually travelled around the continent. Others just gathered stories from those who had been to Africa.

As more books about Africa appeared, the fame of the kingdoms spread and Europeans began to visit the continent. First came the Portuguese in the 1400s. Then other Europeans such as the French, Dutch and British followed. They built forts along the coast and traded with the Africans. But few Europeans actually travelled into the heart of the country and because they knew so little about Africa they called it the Dark Continent.

Exploring This Book

This book is divided into four sections. The first section deals with the history of Africa to the 1400s, and the second section takes the history up to the 1800s. Within each time period, we deal with different regions of Africa separately. The last two sections deal with European explorers who visited Africa from the late 1700s onwards and Africa as it is today.

This book is the story of Africa and her visitors.

The Beginnings of History

The Sahara Desert was once a lush, green land. This rock painting was made by people who lived there thousands of years ago.

The Nok culture

The Stone Age

Scientists now believe that the very first human beings lived in Africa two million years ago. Because the early humans used stone tools as hunting weapons, this period of history is known as the Stone Age. People lived in small groups, moving about from place to place in search of food. People lived in this way for many thousands of years (until about ten thousand years ago). Stone Age people learnt how to farm and keep animals. They started building permanent homes, growing rice and wheat and other grains, and keeping goats, sheep and cattle for food. Their numbers increased because there was enough food to feed everyone and they even built fires to keep themselves warm.

The Nok culture in western Africa lasted from 500 BCE to 200 CE. The people of Nok made beautiful terracotta sculptures of human heads and animals.

The Iron Age

The next great discovery was how to make tools and weapons out of iron. Iron hoes and axes were much stronger than the old stone ones, and could be used to clear large areas of land for farming. This time is known as the Iron Age and first developed in Africa from about 6000 BCE.

An ancient Egyptian wall painting in a tomb.

Early Civilizations

Ancient Egypt was one of the world's first great civilizations. It developed along the banks of the River Nile around 3000 BCE and flourished for over two thousand years. The Egyptians produced the first 365-day calendar, developed basic arithmetic and invented a form of picture-writing called hieroglyphics. They built great temples and buried their rulers in massive tombs called pyramids. Ancient Egypt survived longer than any other known civilization and even conquered Nubia, a region of the Upper Nile. Around 1000 BCE, the Nubians broke away and formed their own kingdom which was called Kush. The Kush civilization survived until 350 CE and was a centre of art, learning and trade.

The Trans-Saharan Trade

As more and more food was produced, people began to have special jobs. Some of them were responsible for providing the food while others just made tools and weapons. In time, people who lived in one community began to sell any extra goods they had to neighbours. Some people travelled over great distances to trade. The North African **Berbers** travelled south across the desert to sell goods to the people of West Africa. Because the Berbers travelled through the Sahara Desert this trading became known as the trans-Saharan trade. No one knows when this trading began; some people say that as long as there have been people in Africa there has been trade.

Journeying Through the Desert

The trans-Saharan trade thrived for over two thousand years only decreasing in the last century. The Berbers loaded up about one thousand camels and travelled 2,400 kilometres across the desert. The journey usually took three months to complete and was fraught with dangers. Some merchants lost their way in the vast desert and died of thirst. Others got caught up in fierce sandstorms. When they finally got to the trading towns south of the desert, the Berbers **bartered** their salt and copper for gold and **kola nuts**.

The Growth of Empires

The people who lived at each end of the trans-Saharan trade routes were very fortunate. They were able to take part in the lucrative trade and become rich. Each town or village began to select kings and form themselves into states. As trade expanded, the states grew even more powerful and started to conquer their weaker neighbours. Eventually, the states south of the Sahara grew into large and wealthy empires such as Ghana and Mali.

A *camel train crossing the Sahara Desert in southern Algeria.*

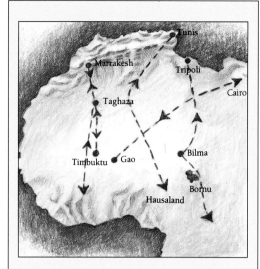

Routes Across the Sahara

At the height of the trans-Saharan trade, there were three main routes that crossed the desert and ended at important trading cities. One route was from Marrakesh to the salt-mines of Taghaza. From there salt and copper were carried to the ancient Ghana Empire and Timbuktu. The second route ran from Tunis to Hausaland and Gao. The last one went from Tripoli to the salt-mines of Bilma, and then on to the ancient Bornu Empire. Both of these routes carried salt and copper. Salt was very important as it was used for cooking and for preserving meat in the hot climate. There were other secondary routes that crossed the main ones. For example, there was a **caravan** trail all the way from Cairo in the east to Gao in the west.

Salt pans in the Sahara at Teguidda, Niger.

2 Africa to the 1400s

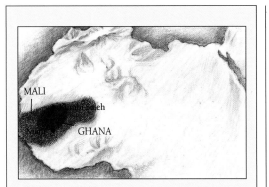

The Land of Gold

Ghana was the first great empire in West Africa. It began as a small state in the 300s CE and lasted for almost a thousand years. The capital of Ghana, Kumbi Saleh, had a population of about 15,000 people. The city was divided into two areas. The king lived in one section, in a palace built out of stone and decorated with paintings and carvings. His subjects also lived in this area, but their homes were built out of mud. Muslims who took part in the trans-Saharan trade lived in the other section of the city. They built houses and mosques for themselves out of stone.

The people of Ghana were farmers. They worshipped many gods and believed that people continued to live as spirits when they died. When a king of Ghana died, the people built a special hut for him. They put comfortable rugs on the floor for him to lie on, and placed food, water and his servants in the hut. The hut was then covered up with sand, burying the servants alive.

Ghana became wealthy because it lay at the southern end of the trans-Saharan trade route. Many Arab travellers visited the kingdom, and it became known as the Land of Gold.

Western Empires

The trans-Saharan trade continued to grow in volume up until the 1600s. The trade was very important to the west Africans, for not only did it bring new ideas but it brought the new religion of Islam from the north. The wealth of the trade helped some people to set up very powerful empires. Two of the most famous were Ghana (see box) and Mali.

The Growth of Kangaba

Mali started off as a small state called Kangaba. Then in 1235 a great warrior, Sundiata, became ruler and founded the empire of Mali. The first thing he did was to build a new capital city at Niani where all his subjects could meet him. Sundiata sent his armies out to conquer areas in the south that mined gold, and Taghaza in the north that produced salt. Eventually Sundiata controlled all the trans-Saharan trade in the area and Berbers flocked to his city to exchange their goods.

The bustling market at Djenné, with the old mosque (see page 9) in the background.

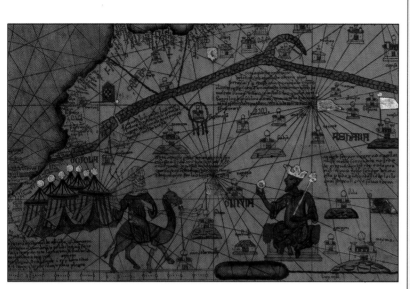

A *European map dated around 1375, showing the king and kingdom of Mali.*

Mansa Musa's Pilgrimage

After Sundiata's death, Mali continued to be powerful. Many good rulers followed Sundiata and enlarged the empire. The next great ruler was Mansa Kankan Musa, who came to power in 1312. He made Mali wealthier by conquering the prosperous cities of Timbuktu and Gao.

Mansa Kankan Musa made his famous pilgrimage to Mecca from 1324-1326. Mecca is the holy city in Arabia which every follower of the **Muslim** faith (see box) is supposed to visit at least once during his lifetime. Mansa's pilgrimage made Mali known throughout the Mediterranean world. Mansa Musa took sixty thousand servants, one hundred camels and three million pounds worth of gold with him on his trip across the desert. He gave a lot of his money away as gifts. Wherever Mansa stopped on a Friday, the Muslim day of worship, he gave the people who lived there money to build a mosque. Mosques are like churches. Muslims go there to pray to their god, Allah. Mansa Musa was so generous that he ended up having to borrow money from an Egyptian merchant to get back home.

Timbuktu, the Islamic Centre

Mansa Musa brought architects and scholars back with him from Egypt. He asked architects to build Islamic schools in Timbuktu. He also encouraged Muslim scholars from other countries to come and live in the city. By the end of his reign in 1337, Timbuktu had become a famous centre of Islamic learning.

The Birth of Islam

In 622 CE, the Prophet Muhammad founded a new religion in Arabia, called Islam. The people who follow it are called Muslims and they believe in one god whom they call Allah.

The first Muslims wanted to convert other peoples who did not believe in their religion. After the Prophet Muhammad died in 632, his followers began to wage wars against people who lived in other countries. They conquered Egypt in 639 and most of North Africa by the 700s.

Muslims follow a holy book called the Quran. It contains passages that tell them how to live a good life. Muslims are supposed to pray five times a day, give food or money to the poor, **fast** during **Ramadan** and make a pilgrimage to Mecca at least once in their lifetime. There are over one billion Muslims in the world and a hundred and fifty million of them live in Africa.

The elegant Sultan Haman Mosque in Cairo, Egypt.

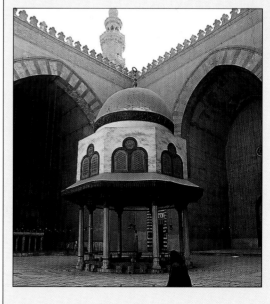

Moving East

While some people were forming empires in the west, others were **migrating** to other parts of Africa. These people spoke several languages called Bantu, and they started migrating over four thousand years ago. The Bantus moved into the forests of Central Africa, continuing until they reached the east African coast around 400 CE.

Across the Indian Ocean

The Bantu-speaking Africans who settled along the coast were farmers who kept cattle and grew crops. In due course they also traded across the Indian Ocean with Arabia, Persia and India. Merchants from these countries had learnt how to sail on the **monsoon** winds, which blew from India towards East Africa between November and March. They brought goods such as beads, plates and silk from China and India to sell at east African ports. The Africans sold ivory and gold, which they bought from people living in the **interior**. When the monsoon winds blew eastwards between April and October, the foreign merchants sailed home in their **dhows**.

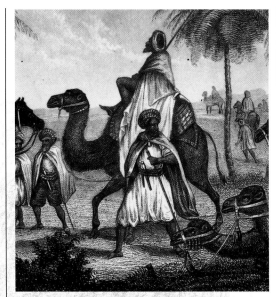

A *detail from a nineteenth century European engraving of an Arab caravan travelling across the desert to sell their wares.*

An Arab Dhow

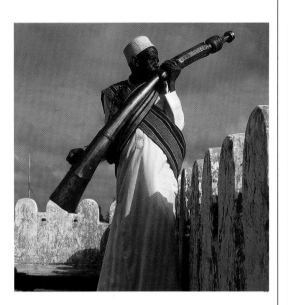

A *Swahili man blowing on a Siwa horn. Swahilis are the descendants of Bantu and Arab settlers.*

A *page from Ptolemy's book,* **Geography**.

Arab Settlers

During the tenth century, Arab merchants began to settle along the east African coast. They learnt the languages and became middlemen, buying goods from Africans who lived further inland and selling them to the sea merchants. A century later, wars in Persia and Arabia forced many Arabs to move away from their troubled homes. Some of them ended up settling along the east African coast and taking part in the trade as well. These Arabs married local African women, and as time went on a new language called Swahili developed. Swahili is basically a Bantu language with lots of Arabic words. It is still spoken today throughout eastern Africa, and is the national language of Tanzania and Kenya.

Growing Settlements

Many Arab immigrants settled in the port of Mogadishu, and it became an important centre of the Indian Ocean trade. But as the demand for African ivory (elephant tusks) increased in China and India, more Arabs left Persia and Oman and settled along the east African coast. Finally, in the twelfth century, a number of Swahili merchants who lived in the north moved to the south and established new trading cities. The most important and wealthy city was Kilwa. Kilwa controlled the Indian Ocean trade in the south of Africa. Most of the houses in the city were built out of **coral**, and there was a huge palace that covered almost one **hectare**. The Muslims of Kilwa built many fine mosques out of stone, and made their own copper and silver coins. Kilwa's power lasted until the fifteenth century when quarrels between ruling families led to its decline.

The Earliest Books

Over two thousand years ago, a Greek merchant wrote a guide for seamen called the *Periplus Maris Erythraei (Voyage Around the Indian Ocean)*. It describes the ports along the east African coast and the trade which took place between African and overseas merchants. The author of the book wrote about a rich, southerly port called Rhapta, where there was plenty of ivory and tortoiseshell. Archaeologists have failed to uncover this site, but they think it may be somewhere in modern Tanzania.

In the fifth century BCE, a book came out which described the east African trading ports. It was written by the Egyptian geographer and astronomer Ptolemy, and was called *Geography*. After Ptolemy's book not much was written about the east coast until Arab geographers started visiting it over four hundred years later.

Great Zimbabwe

Great Zimbabwe

While Arabs were settling at Kilwa on the east coast, another Bantu city was being built further inland in south-eastern Africa. It was called Great Zimbabwe. Great Zimbabwe was important for Indian Ocean trade because most of the gold and ivory sold by Arab merchants at Sofala (a port on the coast) passed through the city.

The Stone Walls

Bantu-speaking people started living around the **Zimbabwean Plateau** about one and a half thousand years ago. The early settlers lived on the hill and were farmers who kept cattle. Then, in the 1200s, the Bantu people built a massive stone wall to surround their settlement. The wall was made out of granite, a local stone that cracks into pieces at night after a hot sunny day.

A century later, the ruler moved from the hill to the valley and founded Great Zimbabwe. It consisted of a house for the ruler with many other huts for members of the royal family surrounding it. All the homes were made out of thick clay and covered in designs. Each house had its own stone wall surrounding it. There were also courtyards and areas where people could cook. Soon after 1300, a great stone wall ten metres high was built to protect the whole area.

People of the Valley

About ten thousand people lived outside the stone walls of Great Zimbabwe and they all had different jobs. Some were herders who moved their cattle from one grazing ground to another. Others were craftworkers who made jewellery out of gold and copper. Sculptors carved in wood and stone, and locally grown cotton enabled weavers to make fine cloth. But the most important people were the traders who carried gold and ivory to the east coast. Great Zimbabwe did not have any metals of its own, so people had to get copper from mines in the north and gold from people in the south. It was this trade that made Great Zimbabwe one of the most powerful kingdoms of Africa in the 1300s.

End of the Kingdom

The stone walls of Great Zimbabwe were a symbol of power and wealth that also gave people privacy. However, in the mid-1400s, Great Zimbabwe was suddenly burnt down and abandoned. No one knows why this was done. But the stone walls were so well built that they still survive today as a reminder of the ancient power of Great Zimbabwe.

A modern-day picture of the ruins of Great Zimbabwe (left). The drawing at the bottom is a construction of Great Zimbabwe at its height during the 1400s. Although the walls were tall and powerful, they were not built for defence. Instead, they were built to enhance the power of the king.

3 Visitors and Traders

The Traveller of Islam

Even before Great Zimbabwe was mysteriously abandoned, an amazing man was making his way across Africa, Asia and the Middle East. His name was Ibn Battuta and he was the greatest Arab traveller of his time. When Ibn Battuta was only twenty-one (in 1325) he started his journey. By the time he finally returned to his country twenty-nine years later, he had travelled 120,000 miles. This earned him the title 'Traveller of Islam.' Before Ibn Battuta visited West Africa, he travelled through Asia for twenty-three years. At first he only wanted to visit the holy city of Mecca. However, one night, he dreamt that a bird had taken him to a dark, green country – the Orient – and so began his adventures.

Through the Sahara

Ibn Battuta returned to Morocco in 1348 and then left again in 1349 to visit Spain and the famous empire of Mali (see pages 8-9). With enough food to last four months, he travelled through the vast Sahara Desert with some north African merchants who were on their way south to trade. It took the party just two months to reach Walata, the northern-most city of Mali. Ibn Battuta was tired so he stayed there for fifty days, resting and eating pounded **millet** mixed with milk and honey.

Ibn Battuta's Adventures

Ibn Battuta spent twenty-three years travelling through the Middle East, India and China. He visited the tombs of Abraham, Isaac and Jacob at Bethlehem. He sailed down the east coast of Africa, spending time at the commercial ports of Mogadishu and Kilwa. While he was in Delhi (India), he was made a judge by the sultan. By the time Ibn Battuta returned to Morocco in 1349, he had travelled through forty-four of the countries we know today.

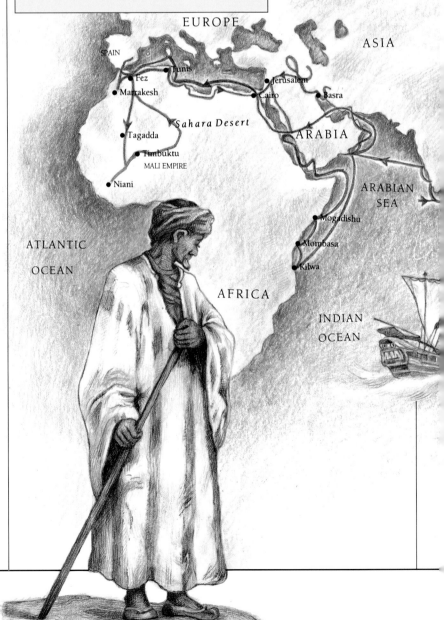

On to Niani

Ibn Battuta's next task was to get to Niani, the capital of Mali. This time he travelled with a guide and three companions. Unfortunately, when he finally arrived at the capital in June 1352, he fell ill and was bed-ridden for two months. When he recovered Ibn Battuta met the king Mansa Sulayman. But he was very disappointed with the gifts the king gave him. Ibn Battuta had heard stories about the previous kings of Mali, and how generous they were with their gold. So the bread and beef Mansa Sulayman sent him seemed miserly in comparison.

Back to Morocco

On 27 February 1353 Ibn Battuta left Niani. He passed through Timbuktu, sailed down the Niger River and saw a hippopotamus for the first time. After resting for a month at Gao, a prosperous city on the Niger, he crossed the desert with a large caravan of merchants. Ibn Battuta spent a few days at the city of Tagadda, and the local sultan sent him and his party two roasted rams every day to eat. On 11 September, Ibn Battuta set off again. He finally arrived back at Fez, Morocco, in February 1354.

Writing Rihla

Ibn Battuta's travels were not in vain. When he got back to Fez, he spent the following two years working on his book, *Rihla* (*Travels*). He worked with a poet called Ibn Juzayy, who took down all his notes. After the book was finished, Ibn Battuta spent the rest of his years acting as a judge. He died in 1369 at the age of 64.

Travellers and Scholars

Ibn Battuta was not the only Arab to travel around Africa. Al-Masudi sailed down the east coast of Africa in about 922 CE. He wrote about the trade between the people of the east coast, India and China. The Arab scholar and geographer, Al-Idrisi was born in North Africa in 1100. He travelled when he was a young man, and wrote about the wealthy Ghanaian Empire. A later traveller, Mahmud Kati, was born in Timbuktu in 1468. He accompanied the king of Mali to Mecca and later wrote about his experiences.

Not all the Arab writers actually travelled to Africa. For example, although Al-Bakri wrote about West Africa, he never left his home town in Spain. Instead, he collected stories from Muslim merchants who had been there.

Sometimes the writers exaggerated in their books. Al-Hamadhani's book, which appeared in the ninth century, said Ghana was 'a country where gold grows like plants in the sand, in the same way as carrots do, and is plucked at sunset'.

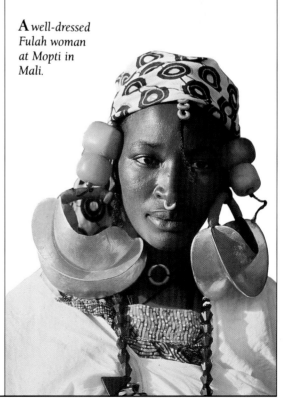

A *well-dressed Fulah woman at Mopti in Mali.*

The Europeans Arrive

Over one hundred years after Ibn Battuta's death, the Portuguese reached the coast of West Africa. They established forts along the coast to trade with people, exchanging weapons, metal utensils and cloth for ivory, gold and pepper. Christopher Columbus sailed from Spain and unwittingly reached the West Indies in 1492. Eight years later a Portuguese captain landed in Brazil.

The Slave Trade

The Americas were full of gold and silver, and the land was ideal for sugar **plantations**. Many Spanish settlers moved there to mine the land and grow sugar. They forced the Native Americans to do all the mining and farming, and almost ninety per cent of them died from hardship and disease. European criminals who were sent to work the land fared no better, and were soon dying like flies from **tropical diseases**. To solve the problem, the settlers began to transport slaves from West Africa to work on the land.

The Expansion of the Trade

As the slave trade continued, Spanish settlements spread out all over Central and South America. Other European nations noticed the profit being made from the slave trade and soon joined in. The English set up trading posts along the west African coast in 1553, and the Dutch in 1593. By the seventeenth century, the number of Africans shipped across the Atlantic to the Americas was a staggering 1.8 million. The Africans were taken against their will, captured either during slave raids or after wars between African Kingdoms. Chained together like cattle, they were led to the coast and sold to slave merchants. Their long, terrible experience was just beginning.

From the late 1400s onwards, many European merchants built trading castles along the west African coast. Cape Coast Castle (below), was Britain's main trading fort along the Gold Coast. It was built in the 1600s.

As early as the 900s, Arabs developed a profitable slave trade of their own on the east African coast. The Africans in the picture are being led to Kilwa, the centre of the Arab slave trade.

The Results of the Trade

Over twelve million Africans were captured and taken to the Americas during the four hundred years of the slave trade (1490s-1880s). The European merchants and plantation owners who took part benefited greatly. The farmers grew crops such as sugar, cotton and tobacco on the wide expanse of American land and lived in splendid mansions. The merchants made huge profits on each of their journeys. The remaining Africans were sold guns, which they used against one another. The imported goods that the Africans received could not make up for the loss of people. The Africans who were taken as slaves were the most important ones – the young.

The Triangle Trade

The trans-Atlantic slave trade was called the triangle trade because of the way it was organized. Merchants sailed from European ports in ships equipped with trading goods, iron shackles to chain people, feeding bowls, and whips. They also took special chisels, which they used to knock out the front teeth of those who tried to starve themselves to death. The merchants tried to fit as many Africans as possible onto the ships, and some people even had to lie on top of each other. The journey across the Atlantic was called the middle passage. It took three to six weeks and was a horrible trip. Africans died by the thousands because of poor sanitation. Packed together like sardines below deck, any disease that occurred spread very quickly. When the ships finally reached the Americas, the Africans were sold to wealthy plantation owners. The merchants then took sugar, gold, silver, tobacco, rice, ginger and cotton back with them to Europe. The reason the slave trade lasted for so long was because it was very profitable. For example, one particular merchant from Liverpool (England) made a profit of over two million pounds in just four years.

This cross-section of a slave ship shows how tightly Africans were packed together. On the right, guns are used to stop Africans rebelling on a slave ship. This did not stop many Africans from jumping overboard and swimming for freedom.

Kingdoms of the Guinea Coast

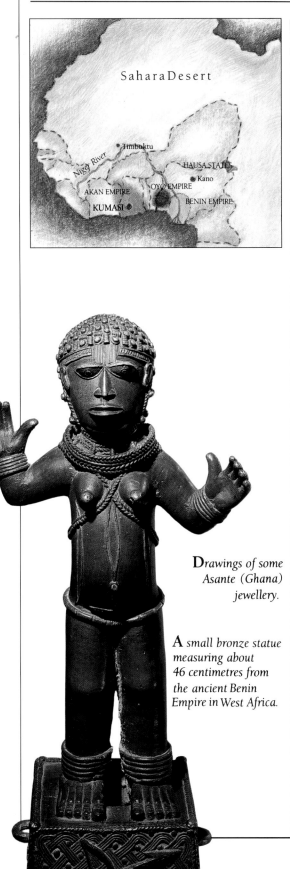

Drawings of some Asante (Ghana) jewellery.

A small bronze statue measuring about 46 centimetres from the ancient Benin Empire in West Africa.

With the arrival of European merchants along the coast, many African kingdoms became rich and powerful. They bought guns from the merchants and waged wars on one another to try and enlarge their empires.

The Oyo and Benin kingdoms (fifteenth to the eighteenth centuries) are famous for their bronze works of art. Further west, the Akan people formed a number of kingdoms of their own, the most famous of which was called Asante. The Asante Empire lasted for over one hundred and fifty years, and when it was at its most powerful, five million people lived in it.

The Beginnings of the Asante Empire

The Akan people once lived around western Sudan. Then, a thousand years ago, they migrated to the south and settled around the Pra and Ofin rivers. As the area became more crowded, a family called Oyoko moved away to the north and built a small town which they called Asantemanso. As time went by, the Akan people built more towns, each with its own ruler. One of these new towns was called Kumasi. When Osei Tutu became king of Kumasi in 1680, he united all the separate towns and called his new empire Asante.

Buying Gold and Making Art

Osei Tutu made the capital of his empire Kumasi. It was a large and important city and many Muslim scholars and diplomats from other parts of Africa lived there. Merchants came all the way from towns in northern Africa, such as Timbuktu and Kano, to buy gold and kola nuts in Kumasi. The Asante also bought goods from merchants along the coast. The Asante Empire became very wealthy and even developed its own system of weights to measure gold dust. Asante craftspeople became famous for their beautiful carvings and sculptures in wood, silver and gold.

The Golden Stool

When Osei Tutu became king of Kumasi, he was advised by his friend Okomfo Anokye. Okomfo introduced the Golden Stool into Asante life. The stool was made out of wood and was partly covered with gold. The stool was supposed to unite all the peoples in the empire under one symbol, rather like a flag. The people of Asante believed the stool had come down from heaven. They thought it represented the soul of the Asante people and that they had to guard it at all times.

Osei Tutu started a religious festival that took place once a year. The festival was called Odwira. Every year, all the different rulers within the empire gathered at the capital, Kumasi, and worshipped their ancestors and gods. They also pledged their support to the king. This festival is still celebrated today and elders wear gold tablets on their heads to signify their importance.

A Warrior Preacher

In the 1800s, Muslim scholars in western Africa began holy wars called *jihads*. The greatest leader of these wars was Usman dan Fodio. As a young man, Usman studied Islam and began to preach to the **Fulani** people in his homeland of Gobir. He won so many followers that the king of Gobir tried to have him killed, but Usman and his followers escaped to Gudu in February 1804. In Gudu he was made Leader of the Believers. This means he led all the people who believed in Islam (see pages 8-9). Usman launched wars against **pagans** and conquered his old homeland within six years. He then united all his conquests into one great empire, and divided it up between his brother and son. After his days of war, Usman retired to dedicate his life to prayer and learning.

Great Kings

Osei Tutu ruled over Asante until 1717. Then his grand-nephew, Opoku Ware, became king. Opoku Ware was a warrior, and in the thirty years of his reign, he made the Asante Empire even larger. The next two great Asante leaders had a massive empire to govern. They organized a strong government with officers to collect taxes throughout the region. But by the end of the 1800s the empire began to grow weaker. It was involved in many wars with people along the coast. It also fought nine battles with the British between 1807 and 1901. By the end of these battles, the British had gained control of the Asante Empire.

Most of the bronze heads of the Benin Empire were made in honour of kings who were called Obas. This head of the queen mother is 50 centimetres high.

The Mighty Rozvi

The first Portuguese contacts with Africa were made at Sofala. This is a seventeenth century European map of the trading post of Sofala with its fort, church and houses.

While the British and Africans were busy trading and fighting on the west coast, the Portuguese sailed around the southern tip of Africa to the east coast. In the 1530s, they sent a party up the Zambezi River to find out where the gold sold by Swahili traders came from. They ended up establishing trading links with the Monomotapa Empire, a large inland empire in charge of much of the trade. By the 1600s many more Portuguese settlers arrived in the area, taking over large areas of land and disrupting the Monomotapa Empire.

Dombo the Great

The Portuguese were prevented from moving further inland by a man called Dombo. He was a wealthy cattle owner who set up his own empire in south-western Zimbabwe known as Rozvi. Between 1684 and 1696, Dombo and his army fought the Portuguese, and finally drove them off the Zimbabwean Plateau entirely. After Dombo died in 1696, the Rozvi Empire continued to expand.

Growth of the Empire

The Rozvi people built themselves a new capital at Khami. Their king took the title of Mambo, and he ruled over the vast empire with the help of local chiefs and officials. The officials were in charge of collecting taxes in different areas – gold, ivory, cattle and animal skins – which they took back to the Mambo. The Mambo had many wives, and some of them helped him to rule.

Stone wall ruins such as these at Khami can be found all over the Zimbabwean Plateau.

The Rozvi Empire

The people of Rozvi were traders, herders and farmers. They grew crops such as pumpkins, beans and watermelons and they used cattle for tilling the land. Traders moved around the empire selling local cloth, ivory and beads and buying cannons and jewellery from the Portuguese.

Magic and Religion

The people of Rozvi believed in one god whom they called Mwari. He had a special place, or shrine, where people went to worship him. Priests looked after the shrines and they were the only ones allowed to talk directly to Mwari.

The Rozvi people also believed that their king had magical powers. Some said that he had a jug of oil that could kill any living person. A lot of them thought the Mambo could make bees fight for him, make rain fall and change the colour of cattle.

End of Empire

The Rozvi Empire was brought to an end in the 1830s by an invasion of warring peoples from southern Africa, the Nguni. These wars spread out all over Central and South Africa, and lasted for over fifteen years. They are known as the Mfecane, or 'time of crushing'.

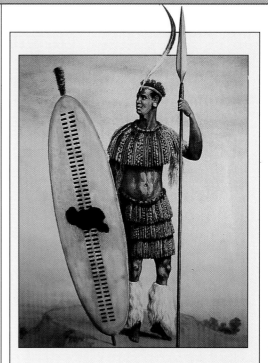

A painting of the king Shaka by Gerard Bengu.

Shaka, the Zulu Warrior

Shaka was the **illegitimate** son of the Zulu chief. When he was young he joined a neighbouring chief's army. He proved to be such a brave soldier that he was made commander of the army regiment. After Shaka's father died in 1816, he became ruler of Zululand.

Shaka enlarged Zululand by conquering many neighbouring lands. He introduced new fighting methods into his army, and even arranged it into fifteen regiments with special names and equipment. Whenever his army conquered a new land, his soldiers took all the women, children, young men and cattle back with them to Zululand. Shaka then placed all the men in his regiments. He made each regiment carry shields of a certain colour and wear special headscarves. Shaka even sent some members of the royal family to live in the barracks. Shaka died in 1828 when he was only forty-one. He was killed by his brothers, and one of them went on to become the new Zulu king.

An illustration of the Zulu king, Mpande, training his troops.

Inside East Africa

Bunyoro
Buganda

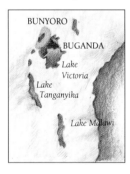

BUNYORO

BUGANDA

Lake Victoria

Lake Tanganyika

Lake Malawi

Further north, the kingdoms around the lakes of East Africa escaped the devastating effects of the Mfecane. But they were involved in wars of their own, raiding neighbouring peoples and taking away their cattle and land. The two most powerful kingdoms were Bunyoro, which lay on the edge of Lake Albert, and Buganda on the edge of Lake Victoria.

An Expanding Kingdom

Bunyoro was the first kingdom to become important in this region. The main occupation of the people was cattle rearing, but they also produced salt which they sold to their neighbours. Bunyoro was divided into several villages, and each village provided men for the king's army. During the sixteenth and seventeenth centuries, the army conducted many raids against neighbours, seizing their cattle and land and making them pay taxes to the king.

A Rival Neighbour

Up until the middle of the eighteenth century, Bunyoro was the most powerful kingdom around the lakes. Then, in the nineteenth century, a kingdom that lay towards the east took over. It was called Buganda and over half a million Ganda people lived there.

The kingdom of Buganda lay on the north-western shores of Lake Victoria. This view of the lake was taken from Kisumu in Kenya.

The king, or Kabaka, of Buganda made his citizens build roads when they were not working on their farms.

Buganda lay on the shores of Lake Victoria where the soil is very fertile. People grew crops, such as bananas and plantains. Bananas were very easy to grow, and any rotten vegetables were used as fertilizers. Ganda people were also hunters who killed buffalo, antelope and wild pigs. They attended regular markets, selling their crafts and crops in exchange for other goods.

Plantains are tropical vegetables which are related to the banana.

The king, or Kabaka, divided Buganda into sections and appointed chiefs to rule over each area. The chiefs were responsible for collecting food, beer and firewood from the people, which they took back to the king's court. Buganda also had trading links with Arab merchants on the east coast, and bought guns, ammunition, cotton cloth, beads and glassware from them.

Ganda Religions

The Ganda believed that certain people in the kingdom had supernatural powers when they were alive. They called these people balubaale, and after they died, people prayed to them for different things. One balubaale was in charge of bringing rain and another helped hunters find animals. There were also many medicine men who gave herbs and potions to people when they were ill.

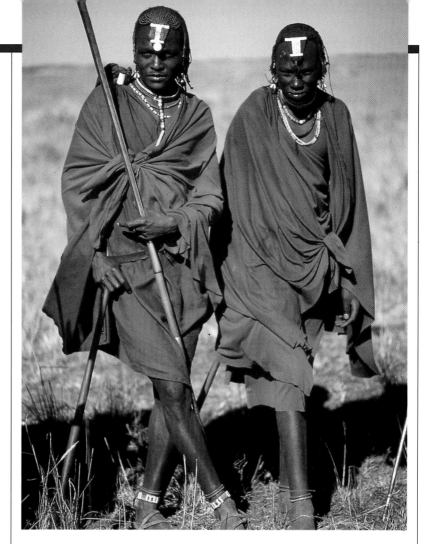

Two Maasai men of East Africa wearing traditional clothing. Maasai men often undergo military training during their teenage years.

The Champion Nomads

The Maasai are a group of African people who move around with their cattle in search of grazing land. Today they live in Tanzania and Kenya. The Maasai were a small group of people in the 1500s, but by the 1800s the population had expanded greatly. The Maasai men were in charge of moving cattle from place to place, while the women did all the milking. They believed in a supreme god called Enkai, and prayed to him through their religious leader. The leader also prayed for rain and made charms to protect soldiers going into battle.

The Chwezi

Bantu people living around the east African lakes were joined by a people called Chwezi in the 1300s. The Chwezi came from North Africa and were cattle herders. Before their arrival, the Bantu had lived in separate family groups, each with its own ruler. The Chwezi introduced the idea of a single ruler, or king, and encouraged the people to grow coffee. The Chwezi built long ditches, called oriembo, which they used to protect their cattle. They ruled over a large area, and their kingdom lasted two hundred years.

5 Changing Times

From Slave Trade to Exploration

Jean-Jacques Rousseau *was a French philosopher who was opposed to the slave trade. He believed that all human beings were equal and had a right to freedom.*

Africans who were *taken away as slaves often tried to escape, and there were many revolts on plantations in the Americas. The most dramatic revolt occurred in St Dominique in 1791, when Toussaint L'Ouverture led Africans to fight against the French colonists – and won.*

While kingdoms were rising and falling in eastern Africa, in Britain a new movement was growing to end the slave trade. There were many reasons why this happened.

The **Industrial Revolution** had begun during the second half of the eighteenth century. **Industrialists** wanted new markets and **raw materials** for their factories. Many factory owners realized that it would be better if Africans stayed in their countries to produce raw materials and buy products made in Europe.

Fighting for Freedom

There were several other groups of people who wanted the slave trade to end. **Humanitarians** in Europe and America campaigned against slavery. They collected stories from Africans about their sufferings and published them in books and newspapers. Churchmen called evangelists and writers such as the French philosopher Jean Jacques Rousseau were also against the trade. In England the fight against the slave trade was led by William Wilberforce. Africans who had gained their freedom joined the struggle, giving speeches about the horrors they had experienced at the hands of their owners.

The people who wanted *to stop the slave trade tried to make people aware of how evil it was. They often printed leaflets like this one which they distributed at their rallies.*

A Great Campaigner

Olaudah Equiano was born in West Africa in 1745. When he was only nine years old, he was captured by slave raiders and sold to Europeans on the coast. He was taken across the Atlantic Ocean in a slave ship. When Equiano arrived in Barbados, he was bought by an English naval captain. Finally, when he was twenty-one, Equiano bought his freedom and began to travel alone. Between 1772 and 1780 he visited the Arctic, the Mediterranean and Central America. In the 1780s Equiano joined the anti-slavery movement in London. Equiano published a book in 1789 called *The Life of Olaudah Equiano*, which described his early life in Africa and the horrors of the slave trade. The book was very popular in Britain and America, and was translated into Dutch, German and Russian. After his book was published, Equiano travelled around England speaking against slavery and selling his book. He died in England on 31 March, 1797.

The Kings' Letters

African kings who were against the slave trade did all they could to stop it. Some of them wrote letters to the governments of European countries. Way back in 1526, the ruler of the Kingdom of Kongo sent a letter to the Portuguese king asking him to stop the slave trade. King Agaja of West Africa sent a similar letter to the British government in 1724. But European governments didn't reply, and the slave trade continued.

Warring Colonies

Africans who were still working on plantations were also fighting for their freedom. In Brazil, some African slaves escaped from a plantation and founded a republic of their own in 1605. It was called Palmares and survived for a hundred years before it was finally defeated by the Portuguese. In the French **colony** of St. Dominique, 400,000 Africans rebelled against the plantation owners in 1791. They defeated large French and British armies and established the independent republic of Haiti in 1803.

Finally, in 1807, the British government passed a law which made the slave trade illegal. But in reality it took over fifty years for the trade to stop completely. Plantation owners in North America continued buying slaves until 1865, and in South America, Argentina and Brazil did not stop until 1883.

The Explorers

Even though the European slave trade thrived for over four hundred years, Europeans knew very little about the African continent. They knew about the coasts where their merchants often traded with Africans, but still had very little knowledge of the interior.

European industrialists wanted to know about the geography of Africa and the people who lived there, so that they could set up trading posts within the continent. Towards the end of the eighteenth century, explorers began to venture into the heart of Africa. They were sent by businessmen, Christian churches, geographical societies and governments. Some explorers who were interested in the wildlife and geography of Africa used their own money to pay for their trips.

Young African children were forced to work on sugar plantations with their parents.

Why Explore Africa?

Mapping the Continent

By the early 1800s, most of the rivers, lakes and mountains of the world were known to the Europeans. But one continent still remained a mystery – Africa. Between 1788 and 1877, there was at least one European expedition journeying into Africa every year. Some were searching for the **sources** of major rivers; others were looking for cities such as Timbuktu; while others were climbing mountains. Some explorers even travelled with Arab caravans through the desert, disguising themselves as Muslims to escape attack.

Commerce and Christianity

Missionaries like Dr David Livingstone (see pages 36-39) wanted to find the main routes by river into Africa so that Europeans could easily move their goods into the heart of the country for trading. Dr Livingstone thought that Christianity would be carried into the interior by European merchants and that the slave trade would end as a result. Unfortunately, this was rarely the case. Many European traders treated the Africans unfairly and it took many years to ban the slave trade.

Mining Africa

Africa is a land of outstanding natural beauty and contains many useful materials like minerals, gold, rubber and **palm oil**. Europeans wanted to use many of these raw materials in their industries and so came to Africa to get them.

Fame and Fortune

Many other Europeans wanted to explore Africa for very different reasons. Some wanted to write books about their travels and become famous, much as people still do today. Some people wanted to see the amazingly beautiful animals of Africa such as the elephant, the lion and the giraffe. Many people came to examine the amazing plants, insects and flowers of Africa and take them back to Europe where nothing else like them exists.

An illustration of Richard Burton wearing Arab clothes on his journey around East Africa. Many European travellers used this means of disguise to escape attack. Some of them even darkened their faces and learnt the Arabic language. This was so they could blend in well with the local people on their long journeys.

Tangiers
Fez
Marrakesh
ATLAS MOUNTAINS
Tunis
Tripoli
Mediterranean Sea
Cairo
LIBYAN DESERT
Caillié's Journey 1828
Barth 1850-55
S a h a r a   D e s e r t
Taghaza
Bilma
NUBIAN DESERT
Nile River
Bruce's Journey
Red Sea
Massawa
Adowa
Senegal River
Timbuktu
Gao
Agades
El Obeid
Gondar
Bathurst
Ségou
Djenné
Kukawa
Lake Chad
Tisiat Falls
ETHIOPIAN
HIGHLANDS
Mungo Park's Journey 1795-97
Kano
Freetown
Bussa
White Nile
Blue Nile
Badagri
Niger River
Lander brothers'
Journey 1830
Baker 1863-65

ATLANTIC OCEAN

Stanley's Journey 1874-77
Zaire River (Congo)
Kampala
▲ *Mount Kenya*
Lake Victoria
Speke's
Journey
▲ *Mount Kilimanjaro*
CONGO BASIN
INDIAN
OCEAN
Tabora
Mombasa
Lake Tanganyika
Ujiji
Zanzibar
Luanda
Burton and Speke
1857-59
Livingstone 1841-56
Lake Malawi
Zambezi River
NAMIB DESERT
Sheke
Tete
Victoria Falls
Quelimane
MADAGASCAR

BRUCE 1769–72
PARK 1795–97
1805–06
BARTH 1850–55
BURTON AND SPEKE 1857–59
LIVINGSTONE 1841–56
1858–64
1866–73
STANLEY 1871 (WITH LIVINGSTONE)
1874–77
CAILLIÉ 1828
BAKER 1863–65

KALAHARI
DESERT
Limpopo River

Orange River

Cape of Good Hope Cape Town
Port Elizabeth

27

6 Europeans Into the Interior

In Search of the Nile

Nile River

A *portrait of James Bruce, the Scottish explorer who spent almost five years travelling around Ethiopia.*

The beautiful Tisiat Falls which Bruce visited on his travels. Bruce stayed with the royal family in Gondar (below).

James Bruce was the first modern explorer to visit Ethiopia. He was born in 1730, and when he was young his father wanted him to become a lawyer, but Bruce hated the law and soon gave up his legal studies. Bruce worked in the London wine trade for a while and then in 1761 he became the **British Consul** in Algeria. He found the place very dangerous and soon resigned from his post. He then spent some time travelling around North Africa and Syria, visiting historical buildings and noting their architecture. But Bruce had one burning ambition — to travel to Ethiopia where he hoped to find the source of the Nile.

Into Ethiopia

Bruce arrived at Massawa, one of Ethiopia's ports, on 19 September 1769. Unfortunately for him the Muslim ruler there was very unfriendly and even threatened to throw him into a dungeon. After being delayed for two months, Bruce was given a guide and two **bearers** to help him on his journey to Gondar. The party climbed over the steep Taranta mountain, and couldn't sleep at night because lions and hyenas prowled around their campsite. Bruce spent some time with the royal family at Gondar, meeting important people and attending wedding feasts. But he longed to continue his journey, so when the king's army set off to fight a rebel chief, he followed them as far as the Tisiat Falls (see left). He described them as the 'most magnificent sight he had ever seen'. Returning to Gondar, Bruce stayed with the royal family for some time. He finally set off for the Nile in October 1770.

On to the River

Bruce first of all visited the **provincial ruler** of the south to ask for his protection. The ruler gave him a guide and a horse, and wished him a safe journey. The party headed south, passing beautiful **acacia trees** and splendidly coloured birds. When Bruce reached Lake Tana at the **headwaters** of the Blue Nile on 2 November 1770, he was overjoyed and even offered a toast to his king, George III. But unfortunately, Bruce was mistaken. He did not know that the real source of the Nile lay many miles south around Lake Victoria. The Blue Nile is a river which runs into the main river, known as the White Nile. Bruce spent five days measuring the river and making notes of the plants and animals. When he finished, he returned to Gondar.

Back Through the Desert

On 26 December 1771 Bruce began his long return journey. He was chased by an elephant and almost died of **dysentery**. Crossing the Nubian Desert was hard work. He was weak and tired, his feet bled, and his face was so swollen that he could hardly open his eyes. He finally arrived in London on 21 June 1774. It had taken him three years to get home. Once he was back in Britain Bruce praised the city of Gondar so much that no one believed his stories. Bruce wrote his book, *Travels,* in an attempt to convince people of his amazing journey. The book was published in 1790.

The River's Source

John Hanning Speke discovered the real source of the Nile. He was born in England in 1827, and spent some time as an officer in the British Indian army. In 1856, Speke and Richard Burton were sent to Africa by the British Royal Geographical Society. They were sent to explore eastern Africa and find the true source of the Nile. Travelling with one hundred and thirty-two Africans and thirty-six mules, the party moved inland from Zanzibar, arriving at Lake Tanganyika on 13 February 1858. Speke then travelled north on his own with about thirty men to help him. By 30 July, he arrived at a stretch of water that he named after his queen – Lake Victoria. Speke thought that the lake might be the real source of the Nile and on his final expedition in 1864 he confirmed this but many people disagreed with him.

The Niger River

Five years after Bruce had finished writing *Travels to Discover the Sources of the Nile* (see previous page), another Scotsman was travelling, this time through West Africa in search of the Niger River. His name was Mungo Park and he was sent by the African Association in Britain to trace the unknown course of the Niger.

Inside West Africa

Mungo Park sailed from England on 27 May 1795, landing on the northern bank of the River Gambia thirty days later. Park made his way up the river to Pisania and stayed with a British slave trader for five months to learn the local Mandigo language. On 2 December 1795, Park set off for the Niger River with an interpreter, a servant and a few horses. The first few days of his journey went quite well. A king gave him a guide and some provisions, and at the village of Koojar, he was entertained with dances. But once the party began travelling again, their luck changed. Park was robbed twice, and ended up losing most of his possessions and all of his money. In the end, he had to borrow some money from an African trader.

The Niger River

On *his first journey across West Africa, it took Park a year to reach the banks of the Niger River.*

The Niger is one of the world's longest rivers. It flows for 4,180 kilometres through several countries, including Mali.

Into Dangerous Country

Park continued his journey eastwards, and arrived in the kingdom of Ludmar on 18 February 1796. The Muslim ruler of the country, Ali, suspected that Park was a spy and imprisoned him in a hut for three months. Park was forced to travel with Ali to the towns of Bubaker and Jaraa, where he was insulted and taunted by the local people. Then, on 1 July, Park escaped across the desert on an old horse. He had no money, his clothes were in rags, and he was extremely thirsty. Just as Mungo was about to give up, he arrived at a Fulani village where an old woman took pity on him and gave him some food.

An African woman gives a starving Park some broiled fish to eat.

The Glorious River

Park finally reached the northern bank of the Niger on 7 July 1796. He was refused permission to visit Ségou, a town on the southern bank, so Park decided to travel on to the city of Djenné. Sheer exhaustion prevented him from reaching the city and he decided to head back to the west coast. His return journey was just as dangerous. Suspected of being a Christian spy, he was turned away from villages. He had very little food and was forced to eat raw corn for three days. Park was attacked by robbers many times and had to swim across rivers to escape. Finally, over a year after he had reached the Niger, Park landed back on English soil.

Park's Second Journey

Park wrote a book about his travels which was published in 1799. Then in January 1805, the British government sent him back to Africa to find out where the Niger ended. This time Park's party included forty-three Europeans, but by the time he got to the Niger only four of them were still alive as the rest had died of fever. Park never saw the mouth of the Niger. While travelling down the river in a canoe, he was ambushed at Bussa and drowned in the river. The course of the Niger from Timbuktu to the coast was finally traced by Richard and John Lander who sailed down the river in 1830.

Mungo Park's second journey into Africa ended in disaster. He was ambushed at Bussa and drowned.

René Caillié (right) was the first European to travel to Timbuktu and back. He made many sketches of the famous city (above), which he included in the book he wrote about his travels.

• Timbuktu

Tangiers
Fez
ATLAS MOUNTAINS
SAHARA DESERT
Caillié's Journey
St Louis
Timbuktu
Djenné
Niger River

The Mystery of Timbuktu

James Bruce and Mungo Park had travelled to Africa to find the sources and **courses** of rivers. But Europeans also wanted to know about famous west African cities, particularly Timbuktu. On 27 April 1816, at the tender age of sixteen, René Caillié left his home town in France to travel to the famous city.

René's First Steps

René arrived on the west African coast ten weeks later. He tried his best to join a British expedition, even walking 480 kilometres to meet them at Gorée. But he was so tired by the time he got there that a French soldier persuaded him to return to Guadeloupe. René worked there for a while, reading about the adventures of other explorers and longing to return to Africa. In 1818, René was back in West Africa. He joined another expedition but was unprepared for the harsh desert journey. Falling ill at Bakel, he returned to the west coast and sailed back to France.

A Third Try

René spent his time in France working for a firm of wine merchants. In 1824, just after his twenty-fourth birthday, he sailed again to West Africa. This time he decided that he would travel on his own and pretend to be an Egyptian Arab. First of all he needed to find out about the Muslim religion and so René travelled inland to live with a group of Muslims to learn as much as he could about Islam.

Timbuktu Beckons

Back in St. Louis (in Senegal), René worked as a manager of an **indigo** factory, saving all his money to buy gifts to use on his journey in exchange for food and shelter. Finally, in March 1827, René put on his Arab clothes and set off towards Timbuktu. By the time he arrived at Tiéme five months later (halfway to Timbuktu) René was suffering from **scurvy**. An old woman in the city looked after him, forcing him to drink **rice water** twice a day. René recovered slowly but it was not until January 1828 that he was ready to continue his journey. He joined a caravan on its way to the city of Djenné. From Djenné he sailed on to Timbuktu, arriving at the city on 20 April 1828.

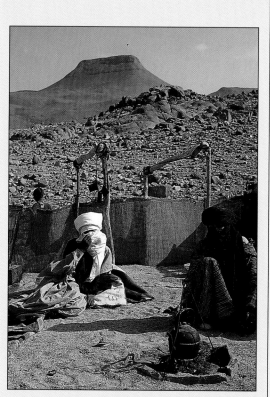

Tuaregs are the largest group of nomads who live in the Sahara Desert. They are descendants of people who originally lived in Libya over two thousand years ago. Today, they number over 300,000. Tuaregs wear loose clothes to keep them cool, and the men wear turbans which they wrap around their heads and across their faces. The turban forms a veil, and only their eyes can be seen. This protects them from the desert wind and sandstorms.

René Caillié lived in a house like this when he stayed in Timbuktu.

Back to France

René was disappointed with Timbuktu. It was not as grand as he had expected but nevertheless he stayed in the city for a month before returning to France. This time he travelled with a caravan of 1,400 camels and four hundred Arab merchants through the desert. Throughout the crossing René kept dreaming about water. But he made it, and by September 1828 René was in Morocco. From there he travelled on to France, arriving there in October of the same year. It had taken him almost a year to get to Timbuktu, and René had travelled over half of the 2,400 kilometre journey on foot. Back in Paris, René was honoured by the Geographical Society of Paris and given a prize of 10,000 francs for being the first European to return from Timbuktu alive.

Earlier Visitors

Leo Africanus (1492-1552) was born in Granada. He was a Muslim who spent time travelling around Africa and the Middle East. In 1518, he was captured by pirates and taken to Rome (Italy). Pope Leo X was so impressed with the traveller's knowledge that he set him free, converted him to Christianity and baptised him 'Leo'. Leo Africanus decided to travel to West Africa. He wanted to see Timbuktu because he had heard that all the roofs there were made out of gold. After visiting the city, Leo returned to Italy where he wrote a book about his travels.

Barth made sketches of all the cities he visited. This one was drawn by him in the mid-1800s, and shows the city of Kano.

The Travelling Scholar

Twenty-five years after René Caillié's journey, another European explorer visited the city of Timbuktu. He was a German scholar called Heinrich Barth. Born in Hamburg in 1821, Barth had travelled widely around the Mediterranean before the British government asked him to join an expedition in Central Africa to encourage trade and to suppress the slave trade in the interior.

The Journey Begins

The expedition left Tripoli on 24 March 1850 and made slow progress across the desert. In August the party escaped a band of robbers, who managed to steal a few of their camels. By the time the expedition arrived at Tintellust in September, everyone was in need of a rest. Barth spent a month there before setting out on his own for Agades. Agades was an important starting point on one of the trade routes in the desert. No European had ever been there. Barth spent three weeks in the city, walking around with his pencil and sketch book and visiting the mosques. Next Barth visited Gobir, Kano and Kukawa and by mid-June he had reached the Benue River. Barth managed to cross the river with his horses, camels and luggage, and continued until he got to the town of Yola. But the king there refused to let him stay in the city, so Barth returned to Kukawa.

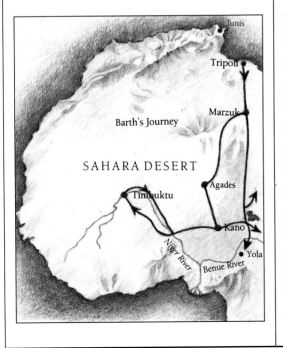

Travelling with Bandits

Barth spent several months travelling to places near Kukawa. Then on 11 September he left for Kanem. He met a group of Arab robbers along the way and travelled with them for three weeks. In that time the robbers stole three hundred cows, one and a half thousand sheep and goats and fifteen camels. Barth returned to Kukawa in February 1852, and left a month later for Massena.

On to Timbuktu

Barth spent three months in Kukawa before leaving for Timbuktu on 25 November 1853. He stopped at Sebba for two days to allow his camels to rest. Afterwards, Barth hired eleven donkeys to carry his luggage to Timbuktu. Because the area was very dangerous for Christians, Barth pretended to be an important Muslim visitor to escape attack.

Home to Germany

Barth stayed in Timbuktu for about seven months. On his return journey, he followed the Niger River up to Gogo, then continued through the desert, arriving at Fezzan on 6 July 1854. The people of the town welcomed him and congratulated him on his successful trip. He finally sailed to Malta and then to London, arriving on 6 September 1855. Barth wrote about his travels and died in Berlin in 1865.

Barth visited Agades, a city in the middle of the Sahara Desert. The mosque in the picture is over seven hundred years old.

Krapf and Rebmann's journey

Early Missionaries and Explorers

Ludwig Krapf and Johannes Rebmann were German missionaries who explored south-eastern Africa. Rebmann saw the snow-capped mountain of Kilimanjaro in 1849 and Krapf was the first European to see Mount Kenya (1848). The journeys of Krapf and Rebmann inspired and excited other explorers with their sightings of these mountains. The British Royal Geographical Society sent Richard Burton and John Hanning Speke (see page 27) on an expedition to find the source of the Nile (1856-58). Later, from 1860-63, Speke and James Grant were the first Europeans to go to the African kingdoms of Buganda (see pages 20-21) and Bunyoro.

Samuel and Florence Baker were a husband and wife team who led anti-slavery expeditions into Africa during the late 1800s.

Routes to the Coast

Perhaps the greatest explorer of them all was Dr David Livingstone, a Scottish doctor and missionary, who spent twenty-eight years travelling around Africa. He arrived at Cape Town in southern Africa in March 1841, on his way to the Christian Mission at Kuruman founded by Robert Moffat, whose daughter Mary he married. The young couple spent the years that followed building three more mission stations, each one further north. The Livingstones were discouraged by their failure to convert the local people to Christianity, and the hostility of the local **Boer** farmers. They decided to explore further afield.

First Expeditions

On 1 June 1849, Livingstone and some of his friends set out across the Kalahari Desert to find Lake Ngami on the northern edge of the desert. They took an African guide with them and it was so hot that the party could only travel by night. It took them two whole months to get to the lake. The next expedition Livingstone made was to meet the king of the Makololo people, who was called Sebetwane. This time Livingstone decided to take his family with him and they almost perished during the hazardous journey. His sufferings were rewarded though, for Sebetwane welcomed them and was very friendly.

The next time Livingstone set out he travelled without his family whom he sent back to England. He wanted to establish a mission station further inland and arrived at Linyanti, the capital of the Makololo people, on 23 May 1853. Sebetwane had already died but his son, Sekelutu, was just as friendly towards him. A month later, accompanied by Sekelutu and many Makololo people, Livingstone began his search for a suitable site. The party sailed down the Zambezi River in canoes, passing herds of buffalo and listening to lions roaring in the distance. But Livingstone failed to find a site and they returned to Linyanti.

This scene of Central Africa's Victoria Falls was drawn by Thomas Baines.

On to the Coast

Livingstone then decided to try and find a route from Linyanti to the west coast. Sekelutu gave him twenty-seven men to accompany him to Luanda on the coast. The expedition left on 11 November 1853, travelling up the Zambezi River in a north-westerly direction. Livingstone was attacked constantly by fever, but refused to stop the journey. The men carried him, cutting grass for him to sleep on at night and cooking all his food. When they arrived at the Portuguese trading station of Cassange, Livingstone was given some new clothes and a guide to take him on to the coast. Three weeks later, on 31 May 1854, a tired and dishevelled Livingstone arrived at the coastal town of Luanda, the present-day capital of Angola. A ship's doctor treated his fever and dysentery, and Livingstone remained in the town for four months until he recovered his strength. On 20 September 1854, he began his return journey to Linyanti, arriving there a year later.

The journeys of David Livingstone.

British society was impressed by David Livingstone's expeditions into Africa. This popular photograph was sold to an adoring general public. Livingstone stands by a globe to signify his travels. On the chair rests the famous hat that he wore on his journeys.

Livingstone almost lost his life when he was attacked by a lion.

East and England

Livingstone spent two months writing letters and recording his geographical discoveries. He was unhappy with the route he had found to the west coast because it was already being used by Arab slave traders. Livingstone decided to try and find an alternative link to the east. On 3 November 1855 he set off with a hundred and fourteen Makololo people. The expedition sailed down the Zambezi River, visiting the magnificent Victoria Falls on the way. Livingstone arrived at the east African port of Quelimane on 20 May 1856 after travelling partly by river and partly by land. He was the first European to cross Africa from coast to coast.

Finding Trading Routes

When Livingstone arrived back in England in 1856, he was greeted as a hero. The Royal Geographical Society gave him one of their two gold medals and he was received by Queen Victoria. He travelled the country lecturing on his experiences and against the slave trade.

Livingstone sailed along the rivers of Africa in this steamboat called the Ma Robert.

The British government decided to send him back to Africa in 1858, to find out more about the rivers of the continent so that they could be used as routes for taking trading goods into the heart of Africa. This time he explored some of the Zambezi area and villages around Lake Malawi. He returned to England in 1864.

Livingstone's last journey was sponsored by the Royal Geographical Society in London. His aim was to find the source of the Nile which had been argued about for many years. Livingstone arrived at Zanzibar in January 1866, and travelled inland to Lake Malawi with about sixty people. The fifty-four-year-old Livingstone was not as strong as he used to be. He suffered from bouts of fever throughout the expedition and by the middle of February was suffering from **rheumatic fever**. Livingstone sent letters to Zanzibar asking for supplies to be sent to Ujiji on Lake Tanganyika. He planned to travel there to collect them, but local wars prevented him from reaching Ujiji on time. By the time he arrived there on 23 October 1871, all the supplies had been stolen. Livingstone was devastated, and as his health deteriorated, he prayed for a miracle. That miracle came in the form of Henry Morton Stanley.

Stanley Arrives

No one in Europe had heard from Livingstone for over four years, and everyone thought he was dead. The American newspaper *The New York Herald* decided to send one of their journalists, Henry Stanley, to Africa to find Livingstone. Stanley got to Zanzibar early in 1871 and organized the biggest expedition yet – two boats, a caravan of camels and donkeys, and two hundred porters. Stanley set off across the humid **savannah** of East Africa and quickly covered 339 kilometres. Arriving in Ujiji late in the year, Stanley greeted Livingstone with the famous words, "Dr. Livingstone, I presume?" Stanley spent four months with Livingstone, and they explored Lake Tanganyika together. But Livingstone refused to return with Stanley to England.

Livingstone fell very ill on his last expedition, and the Africans in his party had to carry him on a stretcher.

Livingstone's Last Journey

Livingstone escorted Stanley as far as Tabora. After resting there for three months, Livingstone set out again on his last journey. He soon started suffering from dysentery, yet he continued his travels, marching toward Lake Tanganyika. By April, Livingstone could hardly walk and had to be carried by his companions. In May 1873 the great explorer died. His embalmed body was carried back to the coast by his African friends and given to the British. Their journey of 2,575 kilometres was a remarkable feat. It took them nine months to complete the journey.

Stanley finally found Livingstone at Ujiji, on the shores of Lake Tanganyika.

Stanley's Journeys

Henry Morton Stanley made three important expeditions across Africa. The first was to find Livingstone in 1871, the second was to finish Livingstone's explorations in Central Africa (1874-1877) and the third was to rescue **Emin Pasha**, who was under siege from a hostile army.

On his second journey, Stanley crossed Africa from east to west, proving Speke to be right in his discovery of the source of the Nile River at Lake Victoria (see page 29). Then Stanley crossed Lake Tanganyika and traced the route of the Zaire River to its mouth. Stanley's story of a great inland waterway leading into the heart of Africa aroused European interest as people saw a way they could transport goods for trading into the country.

On his third trip Stanley crossed Africa from west to east. He saw the Ruwenzori Mountains and recorded what he saw of the geography of the continent.

After Livingstone's death, Stanley continued his exploration of Central Africa.

The area of Africa Stanley explored

7 Modern Times

Africa is Colonized

Many missionaries travelled to Africa to convert people to Christianity. This is a mission school in the Congo c. 1900.

By the late 1800s, European explorers had travelled around almost all of the African continent. They had laid down a map of rivers, lakes and mountains and met many African people. Explorers published books in their own countries about their journeys, the wealth of raw materials in Africa and the benefits of trade with the continent.

Once Europeans knew about the rivers of Africa they used boats such as these to transport goods around the continent. Travelling by water was much faster than travelling by land.

As the nineteenth century progressed, the attitude of the Europeans changed. They were not content to just explore and trade. They wanted to control the new, lucrative African markets.

The Scramble for Africa

In 1884, the European powers held an international conference in Berlin. It was called the West African Conference. During the meeting the European powers decided who would control which parts of the continent. Thirty years later, nearly all of Africa had been colonized. The 'scramble' for Africa was over.

The Missionaries

Along with trade and politics, religion also played a major role in shaping the development of Africa. Using the newly developed steamships to travel up the rivers of Africa into the interior, Christian missionaries penetrated further than ever before. They also used a new drug, quinine, to help fight the **fatal** disease, malaria.

Gold mining in South Africa in 1888.

Resistance in Africa

Resistance to colonization was widespread throughout Africa. The European powers had to fight many bloody battles with the armies of existing African nations to take over the continent. It was generally one-sided. The Europeans had machine guns which were much better weapons than the outdated guns of the Africans.

However, there were notable successes for some African kingdoms. The Zulus wiped out an entire British regiment in 1879 in South Africa. They had old-fashioned weapons but used the element of surprise and weight of numbers to defeat the British.

The Partition of Africa

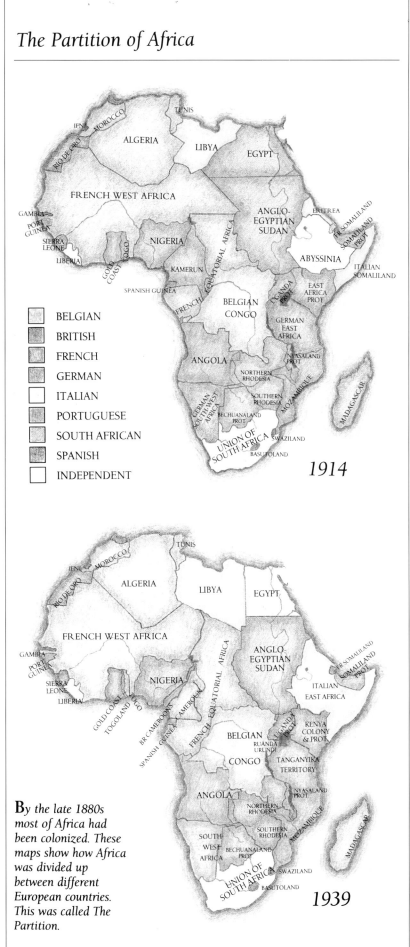

BELGIAN
BRITISH
FRENCH
GERMAN
ITALIAN
PORTUGUESE
SOUTH AFRICAN
SPANISH
INDEPENDENT

1914

By the late 1880s most of Africa had been colonized. These maps show how Africa was divided up between different European countries. This was called The Partition.

1939

41

Africa Today

From the 1880s Africa, with the exception of Ethiopia and Liberia, came under the control of European countries whose main interest was to exploit its natural wealth. Some of Africa's current problems were inherited from her colonial years. For example, before Africa was taken over, there were many different groups living within it. European colonial powers divided Africa up, ignoring the different cultures and languages within the continent. This has led to tension between the different groups.

Towards Independence

In the long term, the introduction of European languages and education enabled Africans to demand the rights Europeans had for themselves. Many went to Europe and the US to study. The first Pan-African Congress was held in London in 1900 and five more followed in Paris, Brussels, New York and Manchester. Africa's future

Prolonged fighting, as here in Eritrea, destroys buildings, orphans children, disrupts schooling and prevents planning for the future.

Jomo Kenyatta, Kenya's first Prime Minister, studied anthropology in London.

leaders used these to plan for independence. World War II so weakened Britain and France, the main colonial powers, that they gave up control of their African colonies by the 1960s.

After Independence

Colonial rule introduced western technology and medicine but what it left behind was often unhelpful. Roads and railways, for example, were built to take exports out rather than to link different regions together. Most new countries were desperately short of trained managers, engineers, doctors and teachers. Traditional problems remain unsolved, and malaria is still a major killer in Namibia, Swaziland and Zimbabwe.

W. E. B. Du Bois was an American historian and sociologist (1868-1963). He devoted much of his life to the struggle against racial prejudice in America and Africa.

Modern-Day Africa

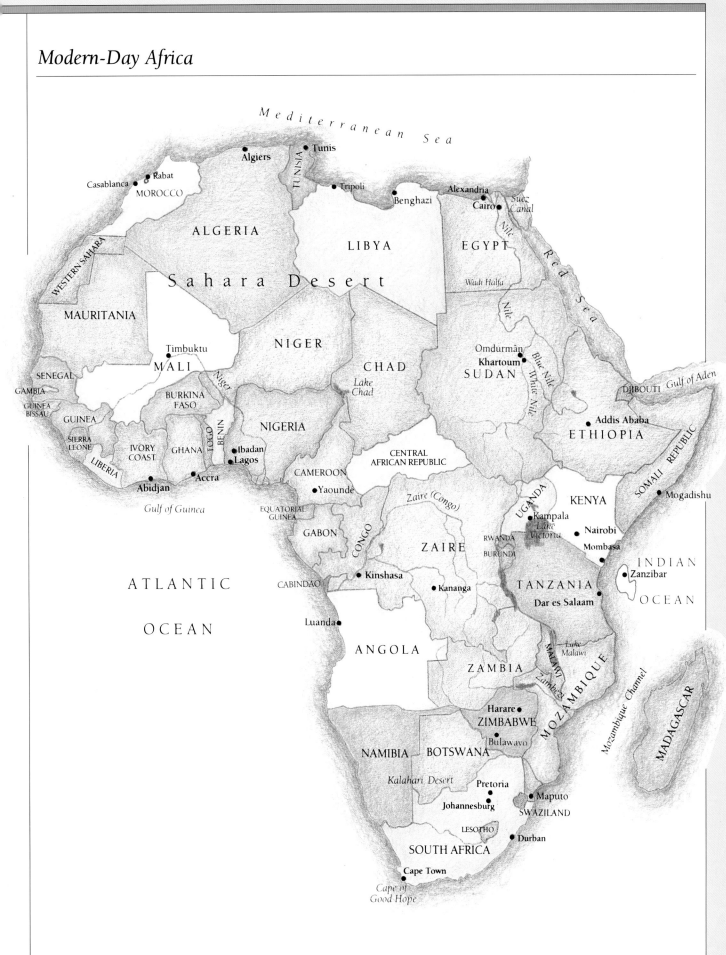

Mediterranean Sea

Algiers
Tunis
TUNISIA
Casablanca • Rabat
MOROCCO
Tripoli
Benghazi
Alexandria
Cairo
Suez Canal

WESTERN SAHARA
ALGERIA
LIBYA
EGYPT
Nile

Wadi Halfa

MAURITANIA
Sahara Desert
NIGER
CHAD
Nile

Timbuktu
MALI
SUDAN
Omdurmân
Khartoum
Blue Nile
White Nile

SENEGAL
GAMBIA
GUINEA BISSAU
GUINEA
BURKINA FASO
Lake Chad
DJIBOUTI *Gulf of Aden*

SIERRA LEONE
IVORY COAST
GHANA
TOGO
BENIN
NIGERIA
Ibadan
Lagos
Addis Ababa
ETHIOPIA
SOMALI REPUBLIC

LIBERIA
Abidjan
Accra
CAMEROON
CENTRAL AFRICAN REPUBLIC
Mogadishu

Gulf of Guinea
Yaoundé
EQUATORIAL GUINEA
Zaire (Congo)
UGANDA
Kampala
Lake Victoria
KENYA
Nairobi
Mombasa

GABON
CONGO
ZAIRE
RWANDA
BURUNDI
INDIAN OCEAN

ATLANTIC OCEAN
CABINDA
Kinshasa
Kananga
TANZANIA
Zanzibar
Dar es Salaam

Luanda
Lake Malawi
MALAWI
Zambezi
Mozambique Channel
MADAGASCAR

ANGOLA
ZAMBIA
MOZAMBIQUE

Harare
ZIMBABWE
Bulawayo

NAMIBIA
BOTSWANA

Kalahari Desert
Pretoria
Maputo
Johannesburg
SWAZILAND

LESOTHO
Durban
SOUTH AFRICA
Cape Town
Cape of Good Hope

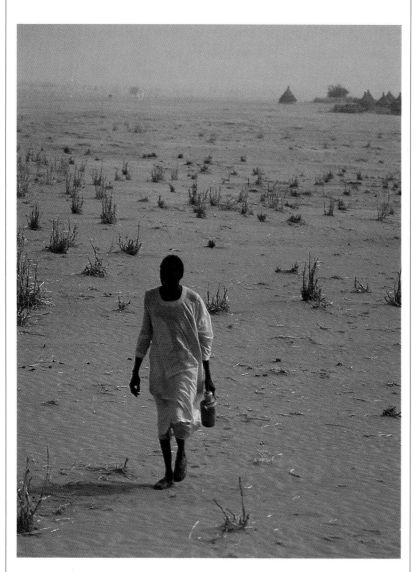

In 2002, 13,000,000 were at risk of starvation across southern Africa.

New Problems

Several countries are now less prosperous than they were at independence as a result of war, government mismanagement, drought and the pressure of rising populations. Resources have been no guarantee of prosperity. The Democratic Republic of Congo, rich in oil, timber, gold, diamonds and other minerals, was looted for thirty years by its dictator, Mobutu. It was then devastated by a civil war which sucked in armies from five neighbouring countries and was responsible for the deaths of 2.5 million people from fighting, famine and disease. Civil war in Mozambique (1977-92) left one million dead and a countryside littered with undetected land-mines. In Angola there was a similar civil war (1975-2002). Civil wars in Liberia (1989-96), Sierra Leone (1991-2002) and Somalia (since 1991) drove millions of refugees into neighbouring countries. Tribal hatreds between the Hutu and Tutsi peoples led to massacres killing 200,000 in Burundi and 800,000 in Rwanda. Hostility between Muslims and Christians has led to riots and deaths in Chad, Ivory Coast, Nigeria, Ghana and Kenya and two long civil wars in Sudan. Soldiers have seized power from elected governments in over a dozen countries.

Apart from war, the two greatest threats to development are environmental damage and AIDS. Desertification, where agricultural land is taken over by desert, and deforestation have made natural droughts much worse resulting in massive famines.

There are now 25 million sufferers of AIDS in Africa. AIDS threatens the political stability and economic success of Malawi, which has avoided civil war. It is a serious problem in Uganda, which has recovered from its civil war, and even South Africa, the continent's richest country. Several African leaders have made tackling AIDS their top priority

There are success stories. Gabon, has avoided conflict and prospered from newly discovered oil. Tourism already offers a new source of income to Gambia, Kenya and South Africa.

Modern Visitors and New Explorers

In spite of the problems, Africa remains a vast and beautiful continent. It attracts millions of visitors every year, eager to experience the rich diverse wildlife and extraordinary landscape.

Apart from tourists, Africa also attracts modern explorers: archaeologists and anthropologists. Anthropologists study the way people live while archaeologists study the objects and remains of ancient peoples to find out how they lived thousands of years ago.

Human Bones

One modern explorer who did a great deal of work in eastern Africa was Louis Leakey (above left) who started searching for ancient human bones in the 1920s. Mary Leakey, his wife, also worked in Africa and accompanied him on many of his trips. In 1959, she found the skull of a human-like creature at Olduvai Gorge (see box). It is called *Zinjanthropus* and lived about one and a half million years ago. In 1962, Leakey found the remains of a species that had an ape-like jaw. He thought the species must have lived there over fourteen million years ago. Later, he found the bones of one of the first human beings at Olduvai Gorge. The Leakey's son, Richard, continued their work and made more important discoveries. Because of the Leakey family's work, people now believe that the first human beings evolved in Africa.

A Fertile Desert

Other archeologists have spent time hunting in the western part of Africa. Henry Lhote discovered rock paintings around the Niger River. Some archeologists concern themselves with ancient sculptures and paintings in order to discover more about Africa's ancient cultures. Dr. Ekpo Eyo has found many beautiful paintings and sculptures in Nigeria. Raymond Murray worked in the Sahara Desert. He found ancient rock pictures drawn by the people who lived there over four thousand years ago. These paintings depict rivers and animal life running across the now barren desert.

The prehistoric skull found by Mary Leakey at Olduvai Gorge.

Olduvai Gorge

Olduvai Gorge (in modern-day Tanzania) has been one of the most important archaeological sites in the world since the late nineteenth century. The gorge is a hundred metres deep and several kilometres long. The walls of the gorge have been investigated by geologists hunting fossils and studying the structure and history of the Earth itself.

During their excavations in the 1930s the Leakeys found pebble tools used by the first human beings. In 1958-9 the Leakeys found the remains of prehistoric animals from the same early human culture – including sheep that were the size of carthorses and pigs as large as a rhinoceros.

Africa	Europe	Other
8000 BCE Farming begins along the Upper Nile.	**c.6500 BCE** Farming begins in Greece and spreads to other areas of Europe.	**9000 BCE** Hunters spread throughout North and South America.
c.6000 Use of iron begins in Egypt. **c.3000** Ancient Egypt founded.	**c.3000** Use of copper spreads throughout Europe.	**c.2500** The horse is domesticated in Central Asia.
c.2000 The Saharan climate begins to get drier.	**c.1600** Mycenaean civilization begins in Greece.	**c.1200** The Jewish religion emerges. **c.1500** The use of iron begins in Turkey.
c.500 The Nok culture is founded in West Africa.	**510** The Roman Republic is founded.	**c.650** Iron is being used in China. **c.230** The Great Wall of China is built.
1 CE The camel is introduced into North Africa at about this time.	**43 CE** The Roman Empire invades Britain.	**30 CE** Death of Jesus Christ. Spread of Christianity begins.
300s The Ghanaian Empire is founded in West Africa.	**117** The Roman Empire is at its greatest extent.	**c.320-480** Golden age of Hinduism in India.
400 Bantu-speaking peoples reach the east coast.	**c.542** Bubonic plague spreads through Europe.	**622** Mohammad founds the religion of Islam in Arabia.
900s Arabs begin to settle along the east coast.	**959** The Unification of England.	**935** The text of the Quran finished. **960** Sung Dynasty in China.
c.1200s The rise of the Mali Empire. **c.1200s** Great Zimbabwe is founded.	**1066** The Normans conquer England.	**c.1000** The Vikings colonize Greenland and travel to America.
1352-54 Ibn Battuta travels to the Mali Empire.	**1340s** The Bubonic plague continues to spread throughout Europe.	**1368** Ming Dynasty in China.
1482 The Portuguese build Elmina Castle along the Gold Coast (Ghana).	**1492** The first globe is made in Germany by Martin Beheim.	**1492** Christopher Columbus reaches the Americas.
1530s The European slave trade begins across the Atlantic Ocean.	**1532** John Calvin starts the Protestant movement in France.	**1526** The founding of the Mogul Empire in India.
1652 The Dutch found Cape Colony in South Africa.	**1618** The Thirty Years War of religion starts.	**1607** The first English settlement is founded in America (Virginia).
1680 Founding of the Rozvi Empire in Zimbabwe.	**1667** The French begin to expand under Louis XIV.	**1644** Manchu Dynasty in China.
c.1700s The rise of Asante power.	**1707** England and Scotland unite.	**1699** The French establish the colony of Louisiana in America.
c.1700s The rise of Buganda.	**1756** The Seven Years War begins. **c.1760** The Age of Enlightenment.	**1775** The American Revolution begins.
c.1700s The Maasai spread throughout East Africa.	**1789** The French Revolution begins.	**1789** George Washington becomes the first President of the United States.
c.1700s The European exploration of Africa begins.	**1807** The slave trade is abolished in Britain.	**1857** The Indian Mutiny.
1835-37 The Great Trek of the Boers in South Africa inland from the Cape.	**1884-85** The West African conference is held in Berlin (Germany).	**1861** The American Civil War begins.
c.1915 Africa continues to be divided up between the European powers.	**1914-18** World War I.	**1917** The USA enters World War I.
1935-41 Italian occupation of Ethiopia.	**1939-45** World War II.	**1941** The USA enters World War II.
1960s Twenty African colonies become independent. During the 1960s 36 become independent.	**1961** The Berlin Wall is built in Germany.	**1960** John F. Kennedy becomes President of the USA. **1963** John F. Kennedy is assassinated.
1975 Break up of Portuguese African Empire. **1976** The Soweto uprising in South Africa.	**1972** The European Community gains more members.	**1965-73** The USA is involved in the Vietnam War.
1980 Zimbabwe becomes independent.	**1985** Mikhail Gorbachev becomes the leader of the Soviet Union.	**1981** Ronald Reagan becomes the US President.
1990 Nelson Mandela is released.	**1989** The Berlin Wall is destroyed. **1990** East and West Germany are reunited.	**1989** Tianamen Square massacre in China.
1991 Apartheid begins to break down in South Africa.	**1991-4** Breakup of Yugoslavia.	**1991** Gulf War to liberate Kuwait from Iraqi invasion.
1994 Nelson Mandela elected President of South Africa.	**1994** Channel Tunnel opened. **1999** NATO intervention in Kosovo.	**1993** Bill Clinton becomes US President.
2000-2001 Floods devastate Mozambique. **2000-2001** White-owned farms seized.	**2002** Euro currency comes into use.	**2000** George W. Bush becomes US President. **2001** Terrorist attacks on New York.

Glossary

A

acacia tree: a beautiful, thorny gum tree found all over Africa.

B

barter: when goods are bartered it means that they are exchanged for other goods of the same value.

bearers: Africans who travelled with European explorers and helped transport supplies.

Berbers: a large group of Africans that live in North Africa.

Boer: a descendant of the Dutch people who came to South Africa in the seventeenth century.

British Consul: a British official responsible for protecting British interests in a foreign country.

C

caravan: a group of merchants, camels and goods travelling across a desert.

civil war: a war in which people from within the same country fight each other.

colony: land that is taken over by settlers from another part of the world and ruled by them is called a colony.

coral: is found on the bottom of the sea. It is a growing animal that looks rather like bone. Coral can be found in many beautiful colours.

course: the exact route of a river.

D

dhow: a type of ship originally built by the Arabs, most often used for carrying trading goods.

dysentery: an infection caused by bacteria or similar germs, involving extreme diarrhoea, digestive upsets and pains in various parts of the body.

E

Emin Pasha: (1849-1892) a German explorer and doctor appointed by the British General Gordon to be medical officer and then governor of a British province in Africa. Emin Pasha became isolated by hostile Arab forces and was rescued by Stanley in 1889.

ethnic: a particular group of people who can be identified by their culture, language, dress and customs.

evolved: the slow development that changed apes into human beings.

F

fast: a period of time when someone does not eat any food.

fatal: something that results in death, such as an accident or a disease.

Fulani: a group of Africans who live south of the Sahara Desert in West Africa. They originated around present-day Senegal, and now number about five million.

H

headwaters: the highest part of a stream or river. The water closest to the source of the river.

hectare: an area of land the size of 10,000 square metres.

humanitarians: people who work to help mankind.

I

illegitimate: someone whose parents are not married when they are born is illegitimate.

indigo: a violet blue dye that is taken from the leaves of the indigo plant.

Industrial Revolution: a period of social and economic change beginning in Britain in the 1760s. It involved the change from working mainly in homes and on farms to working in factories and using large machines.

industrialists: people who own factories that manufacture goods.

interior: the name that was given by Europeans to the unknown middle of Africa.

K

kola nuts: a seed of the kola tree which contains caffeine. Caffeine is an important ingredient of coffee.

M

migration: the movement of a community of people or animals from one place to another either to settle permanently or to visit for a certain period of time.

millet: a type of grass which is grown for food.

missionary: someone who tries to convert people from one religion to another.

monsoon: a strong wind that occurs in Asia. The monsoon blows from south-west during summer and north-east the rest of the year.

Muslim: follower of a religion called Islam which was founded in Arabia in 622 (see pages 8-9).

P

pagan: someone who is not a Jew, a Christian or a Muslim.

palm oil: oil that is extracted from oil palm trees. The oil is used in cooking and food production.

plantation: a large area of land where crops such as rubber and sugar are grown for sale.

prehistoric: something that dates from a time before history as we know it began. The dinosaurs are prehistoric animals.

provincial ruler: someone who rules over an area outside a city or empire.

R

Ramadan: a month of the year when Muslims do not eat until after sunset.

raw materials: the basic, untreated materials (e.g. rubber or sugar) that are used to manufacture other products.

rheumatic fever: a disease which makes people suffer from fever and painful joints.

rice water: water that has had rice boiled in it. Once the rice has been boiled it is removed and the water is drunk as an aid to recovery from illness.

S

savannah: the name given to a region of grassland with a few scattered trees. The savannah is very hot.

scholar: a student of a particular area, subject or discipline.

scurvy: a disease caused by the body not having enough vitamin C. Sufferers have dry skin and swollen gums.

source: the origin of a river or stream; the place where it starts.

T

tropical diseases: diseases such as malaria that are found in the tropical regions of the world.

Z

Zimbabwean Plateau: the name given to the geographical feature that Great Zimbabwe was built upon. A plateau is a flat area of land that is raised above the rest of the land in the area.

Index

Numbers in **bold** indicate an illustration. Words in **bold** are in the glossary on page 47.

This edition published in 2003 by
Belitha Press
A member of Chrysalis Books plc
Copyright © in this format Belitha Press
Illustrations copyright © Robina Green
Text copyright © Isimeme Ibazebo

ISBN 1 84138 647 2

Typeset by Chambers Wallace, London

Printed in Hong Kong

British Library Cataloguing in Publication Data for this book is available from the British Library.

Editor: Jill Laidlaw
Designer: Andrew Oliver
Picture researcher: Vanessa Kelly
Consultants: Dorothy Middleton, formerly of the Royal Geographial Society, London, Dr. Kevin Shillington
Series consultant: Shane Winser, Royal Geographial Society, London

Photographic credits

The Ancient Art and Architecture Collection 45 right; Bruce Coleman Limited 22 top; Gerald Cubitt Robert Estall Photographs 11 left; E.T. Archive 17 bottom, 21 bottom, 26, 40 top; Mary Evans Picture Library 14, 33 left, 38 right, 39 left; Werner Forman Archive Limited 6 bottom; Lagos Museum, Nigeria, 15, 16 bottom, 35 left; The Fotomas Index 9 top, 22 bottom, 24 bottom, 31 right; Giraudon 11 right, 24 top left, 32 top; Sonia Halliday Photographs 6 top, 7 right, 21 top; Robert Harding Picture Library front cover, 6 middle, 28 bottom; Hulton Deutsch Collection Limited 10, 16 top, 25, 40 bottom, 41, 42 right; The Hutchison Library 8, 9 bottom, 19 top, 30 bottom, 33 right, 42 left, 44; The Mansell Collection Limited back cover, 2, 17, top, 24 top right, 28 top, 30 middle, 31 left, 34 left, 35 right, 37 right; Peter Newark's Historical Pictures 30 top; Royal Geographical Society Picture Library title page, 7 left, 20 bottom, 32 bottom, 36, 37 left, 38 left, 39 right, 45 left; Dr Kevin Shillington 13; Syndication International 20 top, 34 right; Zefa Picture Library UK Limited 3, 23